Seven Invitations

James A. Prette

Front cover photo by Lloyd Hildenbrand
Back cover photo by John G. McNicoll

ISBN: 9798702995793

Seven Invitations

This book is dedicated to the people of Hollydene Community Church. As we read, prayed, and discussed our way through this material during the COVID19 pandemic of 2020, you stretched my understanding of what it means to be a "pastor" when we couldn't meet in person each week. I especially want to also thank my ministry partner, Randy Hein. We wrestled through this transformative study together and taught each other a lot during that experience. Thank you!

I also want to thank Kara Henderson and Lloyd Hildebrand for their special feedback and editing. After all my edits and rewrites, it's hard to tell who ultimately won the debates about Oxford commas.

CONTENTS

INTRODUCTION

The Seven Deadly Sins (Pride, Greed, Lust, Sloth, Gluttony, Wrath, and Envy) is an ancient list of the most serious and common moral vices that we all encounter. They are often linked to corresponding virtues. Many traditions offer encouragement to combat the vices by trying harder to avoid them, and to better practice the virtues. What if we looked at it differently? What if we paid attention to these Deadly Sins as invitations to encounter the presence of God in our lives in unique ways? What if we welcomed these common visitors as old, uncomfortable acquaintances, each offering a unique opportunity to encounter the transforming work of God's Spirit in our lives?

Jesus was "led by the Spirit into the wilderness *to be tempted* by the devil" (Matt. 4:1). Rather than avoiding temptation, Jesus welcomed the very human experience of being in the midst of temptation, partly to subvert all temptations into transformative engagement with God. One cannot avoid the temptations of sins. But one can welcome every experience of everyday, real, human life, at every moment, as an opportunity to encounter God's transforming love.

The Pharisees complained that Jesus "welcomed sinners" (Luke 15:2). What if we saw these common temptations as opportunities to welcome, and be welcomed by Jesus? The ancient Christian practice of Welcoming Prayer is a way of centering one's heart in the loving presence of God – especially in the midst of difficult experiences. What might it look like to welcome these seven old acquaintances as unique opportunities to be with Jesus? The goal is not to fall for these temptations, nor to shame anyone for engaging in them: neither condoning sin, nor condemning sinners. Rather, the goal is to encounter Jesus in the midst of these common temptations, and to be transformed by God's Spirit through these encounters.

'Welcoming' these temptations is not an encouragement to fall for them. It is simply an acknowledgement of the reality of the presence and pull of these common experiences, while also acknowledging belief in the presence of God and his unconditional love in the midst of all experiences. These 'sins' can be invitations to vulnerably admit our weaknesses and to experience God's transforming love through them. They are deadly because they are toxic addictions that poison our lives. They distract us from centring our hearts and minds in the life-giving relationship with God.

One definition of *sin* is *distraction*. In reaction to the fear and shame we experience, we tend to hide from what we fear or are ashamed of. This is especially true of our relationship with God. In fear or shame we become isolated from the very one who is pursuing us with his unconditional love. In his seminal work on the effects of shame on every aspect of human life, psychiatrist Curt Thompson observes, "*Those parts of us that feel most broken and that we keep most hidden*

9

are the parts that most desperately need to be known by God, so as to be loved and healed. These are the parts that contain our shame."[1] He also points out: "*Unfortunately, this [hiding] invariably leads to the isolation of hiding from ourselves, from each other and from God.*"[2] Ironically, one of the things we naturally fear the most is abandonment. Each of the Seven Deadly Sins are distractions from God. But we are invited to stop hiding in these distractions, and to acknowledge them as opportunities to reconnect with God in new and deeper ways.

These can also work in our lives as deadly invitations in their encouragement to die to our old, false selves, and to be transformed by God's love into the true selves whom God knows, and whom God is helping us to grow into. Our false selves show up in the fear, shame, and wounds we carry. Somewhere I heard a story about Michelangelo pushing a huge piece of rock

---

[1] Curt Thompson, *The Soul of Shame: Retelling the Stories We Believe About Ourselves*. IVP Books, 2015, p. 125-126.

[2] Thompson, *The Soul of Shame,* p. 113, 114.

down a street. A curious neighbor asked him why he was working so hard to move that old piece of stone. Michelangelo answered, *"Because there is an angel in that rock that wants to come out."* God sees our true selves which he is releasing from the stone of our false selves, which are frozen by fear and shame. Curt Thompson says fear and shame are the primary tools *"that evil leverages, out of which emerges everything that we would call sin. As such, it is actively, intentionally, at work both within and between individuals. Its goal is to disintegrate any and every system it targets, be that one's personal story, a family, marriage, friendship, church, school, community, business or political system. Its power lies in its subtlety and its silence, and it will not be satisfied until all hell breaks loose. Literally."*[3] Thompson points out that shame is a neurobiological reaction in one's brain that has been wired into our thought processes through past experiences that have wounded us. We naturally try to avoid experiencing

---

[3] Thompson, *The Soul of Shame*, p. 22.

the pain of these wounds. There is unconscious stimulation in the brain that drives a 'fear of shame' response which is meant to save us from the danger of feeling that pain. But these can be false fears.

These false fears drive us into false narratives and insecurities that perpetuate our isolation from God, others, and our true selves. Recognizing these common distractions, we can let the false narratives and insecurities die within the safety of God's loving embrace. We can also acknowledge that what we are always searching for, even in these common tempting distractions, is in reality the presence of God, who wants to meet our true desire – which is ultimately to know him and to receive and share his love. We can also trust that Jesus himself is the safe place that we need, in whom we can be secure enough to trust God's work of transforming us.

In this journey, we will be considering each of these Deadly Sins as an invitation to transformation. We will look at passages from the Gospels in which Jesus engaged with real people who can represent our own struggles with each of these common temptations. We will observe their encounters with the love of God in Christ. We will ask: *How did they experience this distraction? What were they truly longing for? Where might false selves be showing up?* Then we will ask: *Where is Jesus in this situation? How does Jesus show his unconditional love? How does he welcome the sinner, and invite us into transformation through his unconditional love?* In each passage, Jesus offers an invitation from the deadly sin into a new way of being through the surrender of the false self into the welcome of the true self in Jesus's embrace. We will see how *"he welcomed sinners"*. We will consider how we might welcome the presence of Jesus in our own experiences of these invitations. And we will be encouraged to welcome the invitation of God – to be loved and transformed by him in the midst of our everyday lives.

Each chapter will end with an invitation to pray a Welcoming Prayer using the context of that 'deadly sin' temptation. Contemplative Outreach founder Mary Mrozowski first composed and taught in our day what is commonly called 'The Welcoming Prayer'. Many have found the following common form, popularized by American Cistercian monk Thomas Keating, to be most helpful:

> *Welcome, welcome, welcome.*
> *I welcome everything*
> *that comes to me today*
> *because I know it's for my healing.*
> *I welcome all thoughts,*
> *feelings, emotions, persons,*
> *situations, and conditions.*
> *I let go of my desire for power and control.*
> *I let go of my desire for affection, esteem,*
> *approval, and pleasure.*
> *I let go of my desire for survival*
> *and security.*
> *I let go of my desire to change*
> *any situation,*
> *condition, person, or myself.*
> *I open to the love and presence of God*
> *and God's action within. Amen.*[4]

---

[4] Richard Rohr, *Just This: Prompts and Practices for Contemplation.* CAC Publishing, 2017, p. 117.

We will use a similar outline for welcoming the reality of our common experience with each of the Deadly Sins. We will invite our imaginations to see the truth of our presence in Jesus, his unconditionally loving presence with us, and his offer to help us let go of what might be holding us captive in the stony blocks of our false selves. These invitations to welcoming prayer will be in four parts, with each part ending in an invitation to *hold* that experience. First, you can consider a series of reflective questions. Take your time contemplating these questions. Hold the answers Jesus gives you. Then, using your holy imagination, you can welcome Jesus into your own prayerful reflection on that temptation. Hold that experience. Then you can let Jesus welcome you. This is a very unique and private opportunity for you to let Jesus contemplatively meet you personally and deeply. Take your time with this section. Let Jesus welcome you in whatever way you and he need. Hold that experience. You are invited to let go of the false things we cling to, like your desires for security, control, and approval, and your desires to change situations, people, and yourself. Finally, you are invited to open your heart to the loving presence of God and the healing action and grace that God is giving to you right now. There is also a series of follow up questions and space for notes at the end of each chapter, to carry with you on the journey of listening to God's offer to be transformed through these seven invitations.

Notes:

Chapter 1

From Pride to Peace

Mark 9:33-37

*They came to Capernaum.
When he was in the house,
he asked them, "What were
you arguing about on the
road?" But they kept quiet
because on the way they
had argued about who was
the greatest. Sitting down,
Jesus called the Twelve and
said, "If anyone wants to
be first, he must be the very
last, and the servant of
all." He took a little child
and had him stand among
them. Taking him in his
arms, he said to them,
"Whoever welcomes one of
these little children in my
name welcomes me; and
whoever welcomes me does
not welcome me but the one
who sent me."*

The first distraction we are going to explore is Pride. Pride is a good one to start with because it is basically about centring on one's self-interest while debasing others. It is about comparing and competing with others to arrogantly assert dominating superiority over them. One could argue that this self-interested dominance lies at the heart of all the oppressive supremacies behind sexism, racism, heterosexism, and other ways any human might subjugate another. These are some of the most basic ways human beings have wounded one another throughout history. Of course, pride can be used in a positive sense. One can take pride in a job well done, or in a loved one's accomplishments. A common way we hear about pride today might be in the context of a 'pride parade'. The kind of Pride that is a Deadly Sin, however, is the distraction from being centred in the unconditional love of God through trying to prove one's worth by comparing to and competing with others. It's about the desire to assert one's self and devalue others. It is self-centredness. It is the opposite of centring in

God's love. It is the kind of false self-assertion that is meant by these scriptures:

The LORD detests all the proud of heart.
Prov. 16:5

Pride goes before destruction,
a haughty spirit before a fall.
Prov. 16:18

In their pride the wicked do not seek him;
in all their thoughts there is no room for God.
Psalm 10:4

To fear the LORD is to hate evil;
I hate pride and arrogance,
evil behavior and perverse speech.
Prov. 8:13

In our reading form Mark 9:33-37, the disciples were having an argument about who was the greatest. Each of them was comparing their status to the others and competing for greatest value. One has to ask: "*What scale were they using?*" Imagine – there they were, walking along, with Jesus himself in their midst, and they were spending their energy arguing about which of them was better, or more important. But we all do it, don't we? We look around and compare ourselves with others. We invent scales of ranking. We are acutely aware of who we imagine is better or worse, and more or less important than we are. It is such a common thing that people do. American Founding Father Benjamin Franklin said, *"In reality, there is, perhaps, no one of our natural passions so hard to subdue as pride."*[5]

What we are *truly* longing for is validation. We yearn to be noticed, appreciated and accepted. We desperately want to belong. Ultimately, we are hoping to be loved. Unfortunately, we learn early that to feel important we have to assert ourselves and devalue others. It's as if we believe that there is only so much love and respect to go around, so we try to grab what little is available and shut others out from getting too much. As the English professor and author C.S. Lewis wrote, *"Pride gets no pleasure out of having something, only out of having more of it than the next*

---

[5] Benjamin Franklin, *The Autobiography of Benjamin Franklin, 1706-1757*. The Floating Press, 2009, Page 147.

man... It is the comparison that makes you proud: the pleasure of being above the rest. Once the element of competition is gone, pride is gone."[6] We fear being seen as small, weak, or insignificant. We harbour shame from feeling small and weak and transform that shame into false self messages of *"I am small and weak"*. We carry wounds from others who are comparing and competing with us, giving us many messages that we interpret as *"I don't matter"*.

Imagine that scene in Mark 9. Jesus knew exactly what they were talking about, but he asks them, *"What were you guys arguing about on the road?"* And then there is absolute quiet. They were caught in their sin. They were shamed into silence. They knew they had been distracted from what they should have been centred on, and found themselves feeling embarrassed by this common, deadly trap. Their silence is a sign of their fear, their shame, and their wounded false selves. In their silence they were also acting out of that fear

---

[6] C.S. Lewis, *Mere Christianity.* HarperCollins Pub., 1942, p. 107.

and shame. One way we avoid God is through our pride. The point is not to feel guilty about our pride. It's also not about trying harder to be better. The point is to be open to the invitation that Jesus offers to be transformed in the very midst of this distraction.

What does Jesus do with his disciples? Does he say, *"I thought so – you guys are blowing it again! How dare you be so immature and bad"*? No, he doesn't condemn them, nor does he condone their distractions. He simply asked them a question. When he asks, *"What were you talking about on the road?"* I think he knew the answer. I think he asks, like God asking Adam in the garden, *"Where are you?"* He is asking them to acknowledge their distraction from their true self centre, which is God. Then Jesus sits down and teaches them. He says, "*Anyone who wants to be first must be the very last, and the servant of all."* The one who is the only truly great one says that true greatness is found in true humility and service. I imagine Jesus smiling at his disciples. He loves them so much. He called each one to be with him, knowing all of their weaknesses.

Then he takes a child, enfolds that child in his loving arms and says, *"Whoever welcomes one of these little children in my name welcomes me; and whoever welcomes me does not welcome me but the one who sent me."* What is he doing here? He is welcoming a child, simply as a child, with no measure of value apart from simply *being.* In the first century, children had no inherent value apart from their future potential contribution to their family. While they were just children, they were useless. There was not the same sentimentality about children then as there is now. Imagine Jesus taking that child up onto his lap. He is saying, "*You are my child. I love you, not because of any accomplishments, not in comparison to anyone else, but simply because you are my child."*

This is who you truly are. This is your true self. Imagine Jesus welcoming you like that child. Imagine Jesus picking you up, placing you on his lap and enfolding you in his arms. He is holding you. He is welcoming you, with all your pride. Jesus loves you so much, ins spite of and in the midst of all your pride. He knows your fear and shame. He knows your wounds and your efforts to control your life. How might Jesus be welcoming you through acknowledging your pride? What might Jesus's invitation be to move from the turmoil of Pride to the peace of experiencing his unconditional love?

The way forward is through the peace of humility. What we need is the peace that Jesus offers in finding our worth in him. Humility is the confidence one has when at peace with one's true self, with others, with one's environment, and with God. Jesus invites us into that peaceful humility. We let go of Pride as we surrender to the invitation of humble peace in the lap of Jesus. Saint Francis of Assisi said, "*Holy humility confounds pride and all the men of this world and all things that are in the world.*"[7]   American theologian

---

[7] Paschal Robinson*, The Writings of St. Francis of Assisi*. The Dolphin Press, 1905, p. 21.

26

Susan Annette Muto wrote, "*Humility opens our inner ears. It enables us to acknowledge the truth of who we are and who God is. Only the humble can understand the deep resonance of God's voice in the whole of creation. Humility withstands any arrogant tendency to reduce the world to our purposes. When we live in humble presence, God may reveal to us while we read insights that transcend human expectations.*"[8]

This is a good invitation to start with because this picture of Jesus holding us in his lap is a beautiful image of our relationship with him. Throughout this exploration of each distraction, let's keep going back to this image of sitting in the lap of Jesus. This is where we are most welcomed in his love. This is such a perfect way of experiencing the humble peace found in God's unconditional love. We are God's children, loved simply for being. And Jesus invites us to honestly sit with him in his peace, and simply let him love us.

---

[8] Susan Annette Muto, *Pathways of Spiritual Living*. Image Books, Doubleday & Co. Inc., 1984, p. 78.

Let's pray a welcoming prayer:

WELCOMING PRAYER

1. Welcome Pride:

In silence, ask God to help you remember an experience of Pride. When have you compared yourself with others? When have you competed for worth? When have you asserted yourself, longing for validation and approval? When have you promoted yourself and devalued someone else? Who do you wish you were better than? What wounds are you carrying from experiences of invalidation or disappointment? What secret shame are you harbouring? How might you be believing that you are unworthy of true love? What resentments, frustrations, and disappointments are you holding? What are you truly longing for in your pride? *Hold that.*

2. Welcome Jesus:

In silence, wait for Jesus to meet you in your pride. Imagine Jesus seeing you in your pride. Where is he?

How does he look at you? What does Jesus do? What might he be saying to you? *Hold that.*

3. Let Jesus welcome you:

In silence, imagine Jesus welcoming you. How does he welcome you? What might his word of loving kindness be to you? What might Jesus's invitation be in the midst of your pride? How does he show you his unconditional love? *Hold that.*

4. Now let go:

Let go of your desire for security and control.

Let go of your desire for approval.

Let go of your desire to change situations, people, or yourself.

Open your heart to the loving presence of God and to the healing action and grace God is giving to you right now.

Follow-Up Questions:

How do I experience the distraction of Pride?

What is the deeper need I am trying to meet?

What false self might be showing up?

How might I be numbing my true self?

How might Jesus meet me in the midst of Pride?

What might Jesus's invitation be?

How might I move from Pride to peace?

Notes:

Chapter 2

From Greed to Generosity

Matthew 19:16-22

Just then a man came up to Jesus and asked, "Teacher, what good thing must I do to get eternal life?" "Why do you ask me about what is good?" Jesus replied. "There is only One who is good. If you want to enter life, keep the commandments." "Which ones?" he inquired. Jesus replied, "'You shall not murder, you shall not commit adultery, you shall not steal, you shall not give false testimony, honor your father and mother,' and 'love your neighbor as yourself.'" "All these I have kept," the young man said. "What do I still lack?" Jesus answered, "If you want to be perfect, go, sell your possessions and give to the poor, and you will have treasure in heaven. Then come, follow me." When the young man heard this, he went away sad, because he had great wealth.

Our second invitation to welcome God's love is through the distraction of Greed. The story of Jesus engaging with the wealthy man in Matthew 19 is a helpful one for us to contemplate, so we can consider how we may likewise encounter the love of Jesus and his transformative work in our lives. What was going on there in that scene? In Mark's version of this event (Mark 10:17-22) we are told that the man ran up and fell on his knees before Jesus. Why does he call Jesus 'good teacher'? Why does the man ask about inheriting eternal life? Why does he ask about what he has to do? Why does Jesus recite the Ten Commandments to him? Which commandment does Jesus leave off the list?

The Ten Commandments, which God gave to Israel through Moses, were written on two tablets. All ten fall neatly into two categories. The first four have to do with one's direct relationship with God:

1. No other god but God
2. No idolatry

3. No taking God's name in vain
4. Keep the Sabbath

These first four Laws are about loving the Lord our God with our whole lives. This defines the way we fulfill the beginning of the great **Shema** prayer from Deuteronomy 6:4 which Hebrews say each morning and evening: *"Hear O Israel, the Lord your God is One. And you shall love the Lord your God with all of your heart, soul, mind, and strength"*.

The next six Laws have to do with our direct relationships with others:

5. Honour your mother and father
6. No murder
7. No adultery
8. No theft
9. No lies
10. No coveting

Jesus quotes five of the six listed in the second set to the man. These are things that one can verify by one's actions. One can prove one's faithfulness in keeping these five commandments through public behaviour. In Mark's version, Jesus substitutes the final Law "no coveting" for "do not defraud". In Luke's version he leaves it off entirely. In Matthew's version of this event, Jesus substitutes the final commandment (no coveting) with the quote from Leviticus 19:18 which he added to the *shema* and which we call the 'second great commandment' (Matt. 22:35-40, Mark 12:28-34, Luke 10:27): "*Love your neighbour as yourself.*"

In Mark's version, the man declares his faithfulness in keeping these Laws. The original Greek word for 'declare' here is *phemi*. It means to announce. He is publicly broadcasting his status as a good lawkeeper. I imagine him turning to the crowd and announcing it to them when he says, *"Teacher, all these I have kept since I was a boy!"* He is proudly congratulating himself saying, *"I have done it!"* And he is making sure that everyone knows it. He had all the stuff that gave one status in that culture. He was young, rich, pious, and publicly honoured. Luke adds the detail that the man was "a ruler" (Luke 18:18). He was successful and prosperous. He had all the holy habits down pat. Everyone could see that he had everything that anyone could ever want.

But then Jesus bursts his bubble. Mark tells us that Jesus *"looked at him and loved him"* (Mark 10:21). Then, in absolute love, Jesus tells him he is lacking something. What Jesus tells him arrests him in his greed. Mark says it made the man's face fall and he walked away sad (Mark 10:22). Jesus never stopped loving him. But, in love, Jesus publicly humbled him. Jesus lovingly exposed that man's gaping chasm of insecurity. What he lacked was a heart turned to God. That man found safety in people affirming his success with those five public commandments. But he was avoiding God. He was scarce in his attention to the God-centred first four commandments, and he was absorbed by a Greed that made him a prisoner to covetousness.

Jesus knew that this man was gripped by a stinginess that had him in bondage. The man's life was centred in his fear of scarcity. He possessed the very height of every material privilege of his time, yet he coveted more. He was miserly in opening his heart to let the abundant love of God to flow through him and it seems that he was desperate for public adulation – but all of this was probably coming from the terror of never having enough. This is what Greed is. It is an insatiable covetousness; a deep insecurity; never feeling like there is enough, and so one must grasp at everything with ravenous avarice, while being tight-fisted with others. It is a hoarding of stuff; money, time, gifts, possessions, property, privilege. It is a heart that is petty, cheap, and sparing. I believe it was Indian leader Mahatma Gandhi who said, "*Earth provides enough to satisfy every man's need, but not every man's greed.*"[9] The satirical American novelist Kurt Vonnegut wrote about his country's history, saying, "*Thus did a handful of rapacious citizens come*

---

[9] I could not find a reference for this.

to control all that was worth controlling in America. Thus was the savage and stupid and entirely inappropriate and unnecessary and humorless American class system created. Honest, industrious, peaceful citizens were classed as bloodsuckers, if they asked to be paid a living wage. And they saw that praise was reserved henceforth for those who devised means of getting paid enormously for committing crimes against which no laws had been passed. Thus the American dream turned belly up, turned green, bobbed to the scummy surface of cupidity unlimited, filled with gas, went bang in the noonday sun."[10]

Jesus lovingly exposes that the man does lack something. He lacks generosity. What we are all longing for is the joy found in living in the generosity of God's abundance. Generosity is an attitude. It recognises the extravagant, free abundance all around us (time, space, truth, beauty, goodness), and gives it away freely. This is the abundant love of God all

---

[10] Kurt Vonnegut, *God Bless You, Mr. Rosewater.* Dell, 1965, p. 12-13.

around us. Generosity recognises that there is always more than enough of what we all truly need and enjoys sharing it with others. Generosity begets generosity. What is given away always multiplies. We cannot spend all the love there is. As it is given away, it multiplies in extravagant, scandalous abundance.

Jesus wishes something better for this guy. Jesus invites him to sell everything he has and to generously give it all away to the poor. Mark adds that Jesus then promises him he'll have treasure in heaven (which is ultimately all we need). Then Jesus invites the man to come follow him. Jesus is offering him the gift of generosity. But the man couldn't do it. His greed distracted him from following Jesus by keeping him in bondage to his power, possessions, and privilege. He was desperate for his perception of safety in having enough, but he was simultaneously terrified that he would never have enough. Many people live with this fear of scarcity. They fear there is never enough.

This is another way that the false self shows up. When people fear that there is not enough of some perceived necessity, they might hoard it. But the idea of what is truly necessary becomes distorted with the more we accumulate, and soon we are hoarding so many false necessities that we run out of space to store it all. We also become desperate to protect the little we think we have. We greedily hoard what we can, and we compete with others to keep them from getting any of what we crave for ourselves. This selfishness may stem from the shame of having gone without what we wanted or needed in the past. Not having enough can also lead to feelings of not *being* enough. Having less can make one feel like one is less. Past wounds teach us lies like: *You don't have enough, so you are not enough. Therefore, you better grab more and more. There is only so much to go around, so you must clutch whatever you can get and fight to keep it for yourself.*

We have all heard these deceptions. We have all had experiences of shocking selfishness rising up in our hearts. We have all felt the grip of Greed. The point is not to feel guilty about it, nor to try harder not to experience it. The point is to meet Jesus in our weakness and let him transform us through his love. Jesus *loved* that rich, young guy. Jesus gave him every welcome into a new life of letting go of his bondage to Greed. He invited him to be transformed through the freedom of generosity. Jesus invited him into his loving embrace. But the poor guy couldn't do it. He couldn't let go of all his stuff. His face fell. He walked away full of sadness. He avoided Jesus because of his bondage to so much wealth and status.

The way forward is to surrender to the invitation of generosity. Using the word 'ego' in the way we are using the term 'false self', mid-twentieth century Methodist minister Albert E. Day wrote, "*I wonder if we realize the significance of generosity in the struggle to free the consciousness for fellowship of God. Generosity is not merely a trait which pleases God. It is a practice which releases us from bondage to the ego, and also to things. The ego is strongly possessive*

... Its possessiveness in property manifests itself as stinginess, miserliness, greed ... Because of this possessiveness of the ego, the practice of generosity is very significant. It is a denial, a repudiation of the ego. Faithfully practiced, generosity weakens the ego's authority ... There is no place where the lives of saintly people bear a clearer witness. They have all undertaken the disciplines of generosity."[11]

I remember hearing a story of a beggar who sat on the side of a road with a pot holding the last of his food; a meager one hundred grains of rice. One day, a stranger stood before him and said, "*Give me all your rice.*" The beggar was suddenly so shocked and angry at the audacity of this stranger, asking him to give him the last of his meager food. The beggar reached into his rice pot and pulled out only three grains of rice from all that he had left. The stranger took the three grains and left. The stunned beggar sat in his fury for several minutes. Then he felt something in his fist.

---

[11] Albert E. Day, *Discipline and Discovery.* Abingdon Press, 1977, p. 102-104.

When he opened his hand, in place of the three grains of rice he had offered the stranger, there were three rice sized pieces of gold. For miles down that road, people could hear the beggar shouting, *"If I had only known, I would have given him everything!"*

Jesus loved that rich, young man and wanted to give him everything. He also loved his disciples, who were shocked by this event. He says to them (in what I hear as a sad voice), *"How hard it is for the rich to enter the kingdom of God!"* I imagine them standing there in shocked silence. They must have been wondering, *"If this guy, who has met all the outward requirements, and is so obviously blessed by God can't make it – who can? It's impossible!"* Jesus knew what their troubled hearts were thinking, so he lovingly tells them, *"Children, how hard it is to enter the kingdom of God! It is easier for a camel to go through the eye of a needle than for a rich man to enter the kingdom of God."* This shocked them even more. They wondered who can be saved. Jesus continued to lovingly encourage them by saying,

"With people this is impossible, but not with God; all things are possible with God."

Jesus welcome us in the midst of our greediness. He meets us there and loves us, but he tells us the truth. He exposes our lack of open-hearted generosity, and he invites our true selves to emerge out of the midst of our tight-fisted fears. He offers transformation through the safety of his generous love. The very heart of God is generosity. God is scandalous in how open-hearted he is in lavishly giving away his love. Jesus offers us that love and calls us to transform from Greed to generosity. It is a deadly invitation. It takes a deadly surrender; a giving up and a giving away. It takes a death of our greedy false selves by meeting, loving, and forgiving all of our fears and shames and wounds so that, in the safety of his love, we can let go of all that grips us and receive all that we truly lack.

Let's pray a welcoming prayer:

WELCOMING PRAYER

1. <u>Welcome Greed:</u>

In silence, ask God to help you remember an experience of Greed. When have you experienced fears of not enough? When have you felt like you are not enough? When have you hoarded anything? When have you felt like your stuff was threatened? When have you found yourself feeling like you needed to protect the little you think you have? When have you felt selfishness rising up in your heart? When have you avoided Jesus because of a bondage to your stuff? What are you truly longing for in your greed? *Hold that.*

2. <u>Welcome Jesus:</u>

In silence, wait for Jesus to meet you in your greed. Imagine Jesus seeing you in your greed. Where is he? How does he look at you? What does Jesus do? What might he be saying to you? *Hold that.*

3. Let Jesus welcome you:

In silence, imagine Jesus welcoming you. How does he welcome you? What might his word of loving kindness be to you? What might Jesus's invitation be in the midst of your greed? How does he show you his unconditional love? *Hold that.*

4. Now let go:

Let go of your desire for security and control.

Let go of your desire for approval.

Let go of your desire to change situations, people, or yourself.

Open your heart to the loving presence of God and to the healing action and grace God is giving to you right now.

Follow-Up Questions:

How do I experience the distraction of Greed?

What is the deeper need I am trying to meet?

What false self might be showing up?

How might I be numbing my true self?

How might Jesus meet me in the midst of Greed?

What might Jesus's invitation be?

How might I move from Greed to generosity?

Notes:

Chapter 3

From Lust to Love

John 8:2-11

*At dawn he appeared again in
the temple courts, where all
the people gathered around
him, and he sat down to teach
them. The teachers of the Law
and the Pharisees brought in a
woman caught in adultery.
They made her stand before
the group and said to Jesus,
"Teacher, this woman was
caught in the act of adultery.
In the Law Moses commanded
us to stone such women. Now
what do you say?" They were
using this question as a trap,
in order to have a basis for
accusing him. But Jesus bent
down and started to write on
the ground with his finger.
When they kept on questioning
him, he straightened up and
said to them, "Let any one of
you who is without sin be the*

first to throw a stone at her."
Again, he stooped down and
wrote on the ground. At this,
those who heard began to go
away one at a time, the older
ones first, until only. Jesus was
left, with the woman still
standing there. Jesus
straightened up and asked her,
"Woman, where are they?
Has no one condemned you?"
"No one, sir," she said. "Then
neither do I condemn you,"
Jesus declared. "Go now and
leave your life of sin."

In John 8:2-11 we see Jesus interacting with the teachers of the Law and the Pharisees while they were distracted by Lust. As they used this poor woman as an object lesson to try and trap Jesus, they were avoiding the very presence of God by objectifying her. 'Lust' is the objectification of another for one's personal gratification. These religious leaders literally made her stand before Jesus and the crowd of on lookers as an object to be observed rather than a person to be loved. This is what Lust does. In his lectures on ethics, 18th Century German philosopher Immanuel Kant taught, *"As soon as a person becomes an object of appetite for another, all motives of moral relationship cease to function, because as an object of appetite for another a person becomes a thing and can be treated and used as such by everyone."*[12]

Pornography especially demonstrates the message that women are objects readily available for men's consumption.[13]   American   philosopher   Sally

---

[12] Immanuel Kant, *Lectures on Ethics*, P. Heath and J. B. Schneewind (eds.), Cambridge University Press, 1997, p. 163.

Haslanger suggests that there are four conditions that are necessary in order for person *A* to objectify person *B*:

a. Person *A views and treats* person *B* as an object for the satisfaction of *A*'s desire;

b. Where person *A desires* person *B* to have some property, *A forces B* to have that property;

c. Person *A believes* that person *B* has that property;

d. Person *A* believes that person *B* has that property *by nature*.[14]

'Person A' is treating 'person B' as property – their "desire" projects a fantasy onto the other to possess "property" (or qualities) that 'person A' wants to get from 'person B'. 'Person B' is reduced to "property" to be possessed and used. Part of what this distraction is about is that we long to have power over people and

[13] Rae Langton, *Beyond a Pragmatic Critique of Reason*. Australasian Journal of Philosophy, 71(4), 1993, p. 312.

[14] Sally Haslanger, *On Being Objective and Being Objectified*, in *A Mind of One's Own. Feminist Essays on Reason and Objectivity*, Louise M. Antony and Charlotte Witt (eds.). Westview Press, 1993, p. 102-103.

things. We want to own and control them for our own pleasure. Lust is violation. Lust violates people by objectifying them as objects of one's own pleasure. Often Lust is pictured as a sexy, seductive woman. But it is not really about sex. And it is not just a male distraction. Sex is a beautiful part of God's created order, full of opportunity for love. Love invites wonder and pleasure, service and delight, intimacy and vulnerability. But when sex is distorted, rather than being loving, it can be just another way we use people (and things) as objects for our own selfish gratifications. Lust uses people and things as objects of personal fantasies. Again, it's not just about sex. We lust after things all the time. Magazines, TV shows, and the internet are full of house porn, car porn, vacation porn. We drool over possessing people and things for our fantasy and pleasure.

Another problem with seeing Lust as merely the seduction of a sexy woman is that it places the blame on the sexy woman, as if it is her fault that one lusts for her. This 'blame the victim' mentality is a part of the way we are distracted from love by Lust. The woman in John 8, was 'caught'; trapped by these men as an object for their use – they used her as an object of immorality. They made her stand there as an object to say, *"Look here. This thing is a picture of adulterous lust."* We actually don't know what her story really was. How was she 'caught'? What was she actually doing? How did they catch her? Were they lustfully spying on her? Where is the man she was with? Was it one of her accusers who was actually the one who had used her and then accused her? We don't know this woman's story. Maybe she was willfully engaging in illicit behaviour, but these religious leaders were certainly distracted by Lust.

They were also using her to trap Jesus. They were trying to make him compromise – he could either break the Law or break his ethic of unconditional love. Would he be a liar or a lawbreaker? They were saying, *"You tell us Jesus – should we throw away the Law or throw rocks at her until she's dead?"* Lust is the opposite of love. Love involves sacrifice, service, and delight in the other. Those men were not loving that poor woman. They were not loving Jesus. They were not loving each other or themselves as they used their power to try to control Jesus, this woman, the crowds, their world. We all do this. Can you recognize the ways you objectify people and things for your own pleasure? Can you remember when you have desired to assert control over people and things, wanting to possess them for yourself?

But what are we really longing for when tempted by Lust? I think we are ultimately wanting to be desired by another, to be treasured by someone. The ultimate fantasy that drives the objectification of others is the desire to be desired, and the fear and shame that we are not worthy of another's desire. We are desperate to feel like we are worthy of love. We yearn for satisfying pleasure, but ultimately our false selves crave to possess that person or thing that we think, in our fantasies, will bring us the satisfaction of being loved that we ultimately yearn for. Love is distorted by our false desires for security and control, and the drive to change situations, people, and ourselves. This is because we are full of fears that we are unlovable, or not enough. We carry wounds from the many rejections we have experienced throughout our lives, and we harbour our secret belief that we are unworthy of true love because of our real or imagined unforgivable flaws, so we assert objectifying control over things and people with pornographic fantasies of personal power. Imagining their looks of desire for us and their promises of ecstasy and intimacy, we fantasize being fully naked, known, and adored by another. We lust after being truly accepted, cherished, and finally fully enough. The point is not to feel guilty about our lusts. It's also not about trying harder to be better. The point is to be open to the invitation to be transformed that Jesus offers in the very midst of this distraction.

Where is Jesus in this experience? He is right there. He was there with the woman and her accusers, as well as the disciples and the rest of the onlookers. He was there with all of them, right in the midst of this ience. Can you imagine Jesus looking at each of the people in that scene with love? Imagine Jesus looking at that woman – caught, trapped in the clutches of those desperate men. How did she end up in that terrible situation? How humiliating and devastating this experience was for her! Imagine him looking at each of those men with love. These were the ones who were supposed to know God the best. Yet they were trying so hard to trap him. They wanted so desperately to control him. Why was their faith so brittle? Why were they so brutally abusive? Imagine him looking at his disciples and the other onlookers, who were standing there doing nothing, except maybe gawking at the woman. Maybe they were lusting after her in their fantasies while she stood there in her shame and fear.

Can you imagine yourself in that scene with Jesus? Imagine yourself as each of them: that terrified, ashamed woman; one of those self-righteous, abusive men; one of the passive disciples or onlookers. How does Jesus look at you? How is he welcoming you in his love? Then imagine Jesus crouching down and writing in the dust. We don't know what he was writing, but we can imagine that he sucked all the attention away from that objectified woman and drew all of their abusive gawking on to himself. Imagine how that lingering silence lasted, while all eyes were on him rather than the woman. That's what he does. He draws the poisons of our brutal lusts on to himself. Then he invites us to let him transform us through his love.

He stands back up and says, *"OK. Go ahead. Whoever of you has never sinned has my permission to throw rocks at her until she's dead."* He just makes this profoundly shocking statement and then crouches back down and starts doodling in the dust again. And then there is another long silence as brittle hearts are gently pried open. The honest vulnerability of listening to the kind but deadly invitation to admit our lusts is transformative. In absolute unconditional love Jesus invites them to admit that they are also 'caught' in the distraction of Lust. And the truth of it slays them.

One by one, starting with the oldest ones, those accusers dropped their rocks and walked away. The ones who had been around the Temple the longest, the ones who had listened to the scriptures for the most years, the ones who had read, sung and prayed the psalms for more of their days were 'caught' by love first. They 'caught' it, and they walked away. Jesus caught them. Absorbing their objectifying lusts, he offers the invitation to love; have respect, feel concern, know truth.

The way forward is to surrender to the invitation to be unconditionally loved by Jesus. He accepts us just as we are. We are not an object to him. Rather, we are each a cherished, welcomed, beloved one in whom he delights. After all the men leave, Jesus addresses the woman. There she was – left alone. None of her accusers remained. There was only Jesus and his disciples standing before her. (I imagine the disciples smiling at her as they had just witnessed Jesus put those controlling religious men in their place.) Jesus gives her an invitation. He asks her, *"Where are your accusers?"* She says, *"They're gone."* *"That's right,"* he says, *"And I don't accuse you either. Now go and leave this. You don't need to be caught in the traps of lust anymore."* I think he meant that she was to let go of all the ways she was caught in the distractions of lust and to walk in the freedom of God's unconditional love. Jesus offers us that same transformation through his unconditional love. Our true selves are invited to emerge through his unlimited acceptance. You are the beloved, and you are invited to move from Lust to love.

Let's pray a welcoming prayer:

■ ■

WELCOMING PRAYER

1. Welcome Lust:

In silence, ask God to help you remember an experience of Lust. When have you experienced objectifying or being objectified? When have you seen people or things as objects for personal gratification? When have you fantasized possessing a person or thing hoping for satisfaction? How do you wish you were loved? How have you desired security and control? How have you feared that you are unlovable, or not enough? What wounds are you carrying from experiences of rejection? What secret shame are you harbouring? How might you believe that you are unworthy of true love? What resentments, frustrations, and disappointments are you holding? What are you truly longing for in your lust? *Hold that.*

2. Welcome Jesus:

In silence, wait for Jesus to meet you in your lust. Imagine Jesus seeing you in your lust. Where is he?

How does he look at you? What does Jesus do? What might he be saying to you? *Hold that.*

3. <u>Let Jesus welcome you:</u>

In silence, imagine Jesus welcoming you. How does he welcome you? What might his word of loving kindness be to you? What might Jesus's invitation be in the midst of your lust? How does he show you his unconditional love? *Hold that.*

4. <u>Now let go:</u>

Let go of your desire for security and control.

Let go of your desire for approval.

Let go of your desire to change situations, people, or yourself.

Open your heart to the loving presence of God and to the healing action and grace God is giving to you right now.

■ ■

Follow-Up Questions:

How do I experience the distraction of Lust?

What is the deeper need I am trying to meet?

What false self might be showing up?

How might I be numbing my true self?

How might Jesus meet me in the midst of Lust?

What might Jesus's invitation be?

How might I move from Lust to love?

Notes:
■■■

Chapter 4

From Sloth to Sabbath

Luke 10:38-41

As Jesus and his disciples were on their way, he came to a village where a woman named Martha opened her home to him. She had a sister called Mary, who sat at the Lord's feet listening to what he said. But Martha was distracted by all the preparations that had to be made. She came to him and asked, "Lord, don't you care that my sister has left me to do the work by myself? Tell her to help me!" "Martha, Martha," the Lord answered, "you are worried and upset about many things, but only one thing is needed. Mary has chosen what is better, and it will not be taken away from her."

The distraction of Sloth is usually associated with laziness. This may be the most obvious example, and perhaps the most misleading way by which we are tempted away from centring in Jesus through Sloth. When Jesus visits the home of his good friends Mary and Martha, Martha runs around working so hard to please him while Mary just sits there with the men, listening to him. Martha complains to Jesus, saying, *"Don't you care?! My sister has abandoned me! I have to do all the work by myself! Tell her to help me!!"* Luke tells us that she was "distracted".

Sloth is not so much laziness as an avoidance of doing the good. It is a holding back; a distraction; a carelessness, especially in spiritual matters. It is indifference and apathy. This is one interpretation of Jesus's second temptation in the wilderness. The Devil put Jesus on the pinnacle of the temple and said, *"Let yourself drop from here."* Then he pulled a verse from Psalm 91 out of context saying, *"Don't worry about it. Let it go. God will tell his angels to catch you*" (Matt. 4:5,6). Sloth is an avoidance of taking responsibility for doing what is actually important.

American pastor and author Brian Hedges defines sloth with four descriptive characteristics: carelessness, unwillingness to act, half-hearted effort, and becoming easily discouraged by any possible difficulty.[15] According to the catechism of the Roman Catholic Church, sloth goes so far as to "refuse the joy that comes from God and to be repelled by divine goodness,"[16] Sloth is a sin of omission. In his *Summa Theologiae*, Medieval theologian Thomas Aquinas said sloth is "*sluggishness of the mind which neglects to begin good... [it] is evil in its effect, if it so oppresses man as to draw him away entirely from good deeds.*"[17] The Pocket Catholic Catechism says, "*Sloth is the desire for ease, even at the expense of doing the known will of God. Whatever we do in life*

---

[15] Brian G. Hedges, *Hit List: Taking Aim at the Seven Deadly Sins*. Cruciform, 2014, p. 63.
[16] *Catechism of the Catholic Church*. Libreria Editrice Vaticana, Second Ed., 2012, Paragraph 2094.
[17] Thomas Aquinas, *Summa Theologiae Discovery*. Benziger Bros., 1947, Q35, A3, p. 1795.

requires effort. Everything we do is to be a means of salvation. The slothful person is unwilling to do what God wants because of the effort it takes to do it. Sloth becomes a sin when it slows down and even brings to a halt the energy we must expend in using the means to salvation."[18]

We can be slothful spiritually while being very busy in life. Sloth is failing to do the actual good or best – this is what we mean by the 'sin of omission'. It is a withdrawal of one's self from participation in what may be vulnerable and risky. It is a holding back, especially from God. Ultimately, it is about avoiding God. Martha was busy, worried, and complaining. She had opened her home to Jesus, but not her heart. Martha was distracted from Jesus. Mary was attending to him. Martha was in the kitchen doing what *she* wanted to do to please him. Mary was sitting at his feet, receiving what *he* wanted to give her.

---

[18] John A. Hardon, *Pocket Catholic Catechism Discovery.* Doubleday, 1989, p. 219.

It looks like Mary was the one being slothful, but Martha is the one who is avoiding Jesus, being distracted by all that she is worried about. Listen to her complaints. Hear the fear and pain in her words: *"Jesus, don't you care?"* I think that this is her main difficulty. She doesn't believe Jesus actually cares about her and so, rather than resting in his presence, she spends her time and energy trying to control her sister, her circumstances, and her Lord. Did all of those preparations *have* to be made? And what about her cry of despair when she says, *"My sister has left me!"* Might that be a sign of some deep wounds from a lifetime of being the one who had to get everything done all by herself?

Martha displays some of her insecurities by not being able to speak directly to her sister. She complains to Jesus – *"You tell her! You make her do it!"* I also hear a longing in Martha for acknowledgement and appreciation for all that she is doing to please God. She seems to be feeling ignored and left out. She seems fearful that Mary is getting what she wants

(Jesus's attention), and so she is trying harder to assert herself (her false self) through judgment and complaining about what others are not doing. Sloth can be a fear of abandonment. It can be a terror of not experiencing the comfortable assurance of being in a calm place of safety. That is the opposite of confidence in God's unconditional love. Jesus invites us to trust him. He promises, *"I am right here. And I am staying right here with you, for good!"*

We are distracted from attention to God by our fears, our shame, and our wounds. We are desperate for security, approval, and control. We are ultimately longing for rest. We yearn to rest in the belief that we are enough; lovable enough, good enough, safe enough. We are designed with a need to rest in the unconditional love of God. We are meant to have a satisfied enjoyment of God's love at the centre of our being. We are invited to enjoy a secure peace in our souls in the midst of all circumstances. But our false selves emerge out of our fears that we are not worthy and that we can't get everything done that we feel has to be done. Because of the wounds we carry from past frustrations and disappointments, and because of the shame of believing the many lies that we are not *enough*, we avoid resting in God's love. Also, because of the terror of not being able to control our lives, we often take on the wrong things in a continually frustrating pursuit of proving our worth and ability. The point is not to feel guilty about our sloth. It's also not about trying harder to be better. The point is to see the invitation to be transformed that Jesus offers in the very midst of this distraction.

Where is Jesus in this experience? He is right there in their home. I imagine him smiling at both Mary and Martha. I bet he loved talking to Mary, and he probably loved the lunch Martha made for them. I think he was having a wonderful time being with the disciples and his other friends. He was lovingly demonstrating his commitment to be right there, with them – for good. Ultimately, he invites them all to rest. He offers them the 'one thing that is needed'. What we need is to rest in Jesus in the centre of God's love. We are invited to sit at his feet and let him love us. He is welcoming your true self to sit in his peaceful, loving, calm presence. He is offering you his words of truth and encouragement. Hear him saying to you, *"You are worried about so many things. Only one thing is needed right now. Sit with me. Listen to me. Let me give you my sabbath rest. I love you so much! It is enough, and you are enough. Rest."*

The sabbath was a gift from God for a people who had just come out of slavery in Egypt. It was a radically new way of being for Israel. It was a new rhythm of living into trusting God's care. It was a discipline of living with assurance that there is enough time, money, and love to get all that is needed done, while this time can be set aside to rest in God's presence. It is a gift of saying, *"Enough. Stop. Let go of what you cannot control and trust in what God is offering."* There are many important things to do, but you can only do what you can do. Then you are invited to rest. Jesus welcomes you into silence and solitude, secure in his peaceful, joyful, loving presence. That is where he can replenish you with all that he wants to give you. It is enough. The way forward is to abandon one's self to the invitation to rest in the loving embrace of God's calming Sabbath rest with Jesus.

Let's pray a welcoming prayer:

WELCOMING PRAYER

1. Welcome Sloth:

In silence, ask God to help you remember an experience of Sloth. When have you avoided what you know is right? When have you experienced feeling there's not enough time, money, energy, help? When have you complained about others not doing enough? When have you felt abandoned by people, or God? When have you felt ignored? Who is someone you are avoiding because it is too painful to speak honestly, and directly to them? How do you wish you were appreciated for your efforts? How have you desired security and control? How have you feared that you are unlovable, or inadequate? What wounds are you carrying from experiences of frustration or disappointment? How might you be believing that you are unworthy of true love? What are you truly longing for in your sloth? *Hold that.*

2. Welcome Jesus:

In silence, wait for Jesus to meet you in your sloth. Imagine Jesus seeing you in your sloth. Where is he? How does he look at you? What does Jesus do? What might he be saying to you? *Hold that.*

3. <u>Let Jesus welcome you:</u>

In silence, imagine Jesus welcoming you. How does he welcome you? What might his word of loving kindness be to you? What might Jesus's invitation be in the midst of your sloth? How does he show you his unconditional love? *Hold that.*

4. <u>Now let go:</u>

Let go of your desire for security and control.

Let go of your desire for approval.

Let go of your desire to change situations, people, or yourself.

Open your heart to the loving presence of God and to the healing action and grace God is giving to you right now.

Follow-Up Questions:

How do I experience the distraction of Sloth?

What is the deeper need I am trying to meet?

What false self might be showing up?

How might I be numbing my true self?

How might Jesus meet me in the midst of Sloth?

What might Jesus's invitation be?

How might I move from Sloth to sabbath?

Notes:

Chapter 5

From Gluttony to Gratitude

John 6:25-35

*When they found him on the
other side of the lake, they
asked him, "Rabbi, when did
you get here?" Jesus
answered, "I tell you the truth,
you are looking for me, not
because you saw miraculous
signs but because you ate the
loaves and had your fill. Do
not work for food that spoils,
but for food that endures to
eternal life, which the Son of
Man will give you. On him
God the Father has placed his
seal of approval." Then they
asked him, "What must we do
to do the works God
requires?" Jesus answered,
"The work of God is this: to
believe in the one he has
sent." So they asked him,
"What miraculous sign then
will you give that we may see
it and believe you? What will
you do? Our forefathers ate
the manna in the desert; as it*

is written: 'He gave them bread from heaven to eat.'"
Jesus said to them, "I tell you the truth, it is not Moses who has given you the bread from heaven, but it is my Father who gives you the true bread from heaven. For the bread of God is he who comes down from heaven and gives life to the world." "Sir," they said, "from now on give us this bread." Then Jesus declared, "I am the bread of life. He who comes to me will never go hungry, and he who believes in me will never be thirsty."

The distraction of Gluttony is usually associated with overeating. It is often imagined as obese people gorging themselves on food and drink. The heart of Gluttony is an insatiable demand for more – this can be food, but it can also be anything that becomes an object of fulfillment besides God. In John 6, Jesus was surrounded by five thousand men (plus their families) near the shores of a beautiful lake. Late in the day they were hungry, so he fed them all with the best bread and fish they have ever tasted. They loved that experience – but then they focussed on the taste of the food and not the one who had given it to them. Without thanking Jesus for the great lunch, they rushed at him demanding more bread – for right now and always.

It was out of his love for the hungry crowd that Jesus fed them (Matthew 14:14), but then he knew that they were intent on making him their free-bread-giving baker/king. So Jesus sent his disciples away across the lake with the leftovers, while he hid away on the hillside praying. Later he followed his disciples, walking across the lake. Meanwhile, the crowd noticed that his disciples had left, so they ran the long way around the lake trying to catch up with Jesus. This is the point where our text picks up. When they find him, Jesus says to the crowd, *"Look, let's be honest. You are looking for me, not because you were convinced by the miracle to pay attention to me but because your tummies were temporarily filled and now you want more."* Then he adds, *"Don't pursue that which fills you up temporarily. Pursue that which satisfies you truly and eternally, which only I can give you."*

Gluttony is the craving for more, more, more – and it had better be abundant, immediate, and continual. It is like a gaping hole that is never satisfied. Apart from God's fulfilment, we feel the aching hollow of spiritual emptiness. Gluttony is a way of avoiding God through trying to fill that hole with anything that promises to fill us up copiously, instantly, and repeatedly. That free lunch crowd was only interested in getting their next filling of fast food for the day.

Meanwhile they were avoiding Jesus, who is the real bread of eternal life. I think it is interesting that no one even talked about the abundant (and nutritious) fish again. It's as if they were addicted to the quick fix of the fluffy carbs they craved, but they were avoiding the very nourishment they actually desperately needed. What they needed was God, but they were distracted from God by the tasty gifts of God.

The word *gluttony* comes from the Latin, *gluttire*, meaning 'to gulp down or swallow'. It is over-indulgence or over-consumption. It is an inordinate desire to consume more than that which one requires. It is also connected to soothing emotional emptiness. In his semi-autobiographical novel, *Comfort Me with Apples*, 20th Century American novelist Peter De Vries has the protagonist's wife notice how much food he's been eating lately. The reader knows it is because he is feeling guilty about cheating on her. His wife says, *"Gluttony is an emotional escape, a sign something is eating us."*[19] We may want to escape the emotional

---

[19] Peter de Vries, *Comfort Me with Apples*. Little, Brown &

pain of guilt, shame, and the nagging feeling that we don't have enough, or that we are not enough. It can be 'eating us'. We often fear we don't have enough love, safety, self-worth, or meaning, so we consume more and more to fill that cavernous pit. What we are truly longing for in our gluttony is fulfillment. We are desperate to be fully filled with full-filled-ment, but we gorge ourselves on copious amounts of fluffy, empty, junky distraction. We chase after satisfaction and contentment, but it alludes us because we want it on our own terms. Those terms are that we want more, we want it now, and we want it outside of God's fulfilling love.

Our false selves show up here because of the insecurities we carry. We fear this gaping hole inside us that is never filled. We fear the pain of not being satisfied. It is painful to go without a fix when one is addicted. Maybe we have wounds from not being full or fulfilled in the past. None of us got everything we needed from parents, teachers, friends, lovers,

Company, 1956, p. 167.

children, churches, work, or neighbours. We also fear others seeing this cavernous gap inside us. We feel the secret shame of knowing there is a yawning empty breach within us. We all carry these insecurities. God knows that what we need is him, but that we are addicted to the very things that drive us from him. We need detoxification, and he works at detoxifying us because he loves us, even though it is painful. We fear that pain, but it leads to health and growth.

The point is not to feel guilty about it, nor to try harder to avoid it. The point is to be transformed by Jesus right in the middle of it. That's where Jesus met the crowd who were craving more bread. – he looked at them and loved them. Before he fed them, Jesus had great compassion on them. That is why he fed them. It was a beautiful temporary gift. He knew the temporary feeding would wear off. He knew the bread and fish were going to be the best they'd ever tasted, and of course they would want more right away. But he hoped they would gratefully acknowledge him as the giver of these great gifts – and love him back. He gives us so many temporary gifts; loving relationships, the beauty of creation, the pleasures we enjoy. These all fade throughout life. They are momentary. They are brief tastes of God's ultimate goodness.

After Jesus had fed them, and they had chased him around the lake, Jesus continued to love them. At this point, however, he loved them by not giving them more temporary bread. Instead he told them about the real bread of true life. He gave them a taste of that physical bread to get their attention fixed on the true bread of life. Jesus invites them to enjoy the true bread of life, which he explains is his own body and blood (John 6:53, 54). He offers his true self to them. He says, *"You thought that bread was good? Well I am everything you loved about that bread and more. And as you welcome me, you will enjoy a satisfying full-fill-ment that fully fills that hungry hole inside you."*

Jesus doesn't give us what we want. He gives us what we need. What we need is him. He is enough. He makes you enough. He invites you to be filled with all the fullness of his love. Paul says we (the community of those who welcome Jesus) are *"his body, the fullness of him who fills everything in every way"* (Ephesians 1:23). And Paul longed for his friends *"to know this love that surpasses knowledge—that [they might] be filled to the measure of all the fullness of God"* (Ephesians 3:19). And growing in that fullness, though it can be painful, Paul longed for them to *"reach unity in the faith and in the knowledge of the Son of God and become mature, attaining to the whole measure of the fullness of Christ"* (Ephesians 4:13). This is the fulfillment of our true selves. Our true selves were created to live into that fulness, and we are invited to grow in the satisfying realization of knowing and enjoying that he is enough, and that we are enough, and that it is enough.

The way forward through this is by surrendering to gratitude. It is the way Jesus offers transformation away from Gluttony. American Trappist monk Thomas Merton wrote, *"We do not know him unless we are grateful and praise the Father with him.*"[20] Gratitude is the proper response to being alive. Paul's point in Romans 1 is that all sin comes from humans originally refusing to acknowledge God as God and not being thankful to him. All sin is being distracted from knowing God and living with ingratitude. Gratitude is a gift. It is the gift of freedom to appreciate all that we already have – that we are already truly filled up with all the goodness from God. God has lavished his love on us. We taste the goodness of the bread of heaven all around us. We can pause and appreciate all the goodness, beauty, and grace of God that we enjoy. We struggle with the mystery of why there is so much suffering and evil in the world, but, as C.S. Lewis stated, the real question is why there is so much pleasure and goodness in the world. He wrote, *"The real problem is not why some pious, humble, believing people suffer, but why some do not."*[21] God didn't have to put all this goodness in

---

[20] Thomas Merton, *Thoughts in Solitude*. Farrar, Straus and Giroux, 1999, p. 32.
[21] C.S. Lewis, *The Problem of Pain*. Collins, Fontana Books, 1940, p. 92.

his creation – but he did. And we enjoy it regularly, while usually taking it for granted.

Jesus welcomes your true self into the fulfilling contentment of thanksgiving. American Franciscan author and teacher Richard Rohr quotes the apostle Paul, saying, "*Do not worry. . . ask with thanksgiving. . . and let this peace . . . which is much larger than understanding, guard your mind and your heart.*" He asks us to notice how much Paul says in these few sentences, writing, "*1. Prayer is the opposite of worrying. 2. Prayer is deliberately choosing a state of abundance or thanksgiving, over any entitlement, blaming, or complaining (which come from a sense of scarcity). 3. The peace that comes with prayer is a state of radical contentment that can be sought and surrendered to, despite whatever problems are present. The peace of God does not descend when you have nothing to worry about, which is the merely secular notion of peace as "the absence of war." Divine peace is when you are not worried by all the things you could worry about. That is not just being clever. Trust it as possibly true. 4. This peace is 'much larger' than the mind that needs to understand, label, and explain everything. 5. If you seek this prayerful state first, and this is your pre-existing condition, it will itself put proper limits to the vagaries and violence of both your monkey mind and your manic-depressive heart. It will guard them ahead of time, not with perfect understanding, but with calmness and peace.*"[22] American researcher Robert Emmons has demonstrated that gratitude "*is literally one of the few things that can measurably change people's lives.*"[23] Emmons research demonstrates that a daily discipline of thankfulness will literally rewire our brains to be more centred on life's true meaningfulness. Gratitude helps us sustain a grace-filled worldview.

A daily practice of gratitude is the discipline of being mindful of all the meaningful and satisfying gifts around us at all times. We can be mindful of all the

---

[22] Richard Rohr, *Just This: Prompts and Practices for Contemplation.* CAC Publishing, 2017. p. 115.
[23] Robert Emmons, *Thanks! How Practicing Gratitude Can Make You Happier.* Houghton Mifflin Co., 2008. p. 2.

'bread' around us, and centre on thanking the one who is the 'bread of life'. The apostle Paul wrote, *"I have learned to be content whatever the circumstances. I know what it is to be in need, and I know what it is to have plenty. I have learned the secret of being content in any and every situation, whether well fed or hungry, whether living in plenty or in want"* (Philippians 4:11, 12). Notice that he was content 'in' all circumstances. We can be content *in* all circumstances while not being content *with* a particular circumstance. Though we may face circumstances that are painful, we can be gratefully centred in the comforting embrace of Jesus right in the middle of those circumstances. This may not change the circumstances, but it can centre us in a calm, nurturing satisfaction that can endure any circumstance.

Let's pray a welcoming prayer:

WELCOMING PRAYER

1. Welcome Gluttony:

In silence, ask God to help you remember an experience of Gluttony. When have you felt a craving for more than you have? When have you felt an aching hollow of spiritual emptiness? When have you tried to fill longings with instant gratification? When have you longed for fulfillment? When have you felt the pain of disappointment? What need did you not get from your parents, teachers, friends, lovers, children, churches, work, or neighbours? When have you feared others seeing that you lacked something? *Hold that.*

2. Welcome Jesus:

In silence, wait for Jesus to meet you in your gluttony. Imagine Jesus seeing you in your gluttony. Where is he? How does he look at you? What does Jesus do? What might he be saying to you? *Hold that.*

3. Let Jesus welcome you:

In silence, imagine Jesus welcoming you. How does he welcome you? What might his word of loving kindness be to you? What might Jesus's invitation be in the midst of your gluttony? How does he show you his unconditional love? *Hold that.*

4. Now let go:

Let go of your desire for security and control.

Let go of your desire for approval.

Let go of your desire to change situations, people, or yourself.

Open your heart to the loving presence of God and to the healing action and grace God is giving to you right now.

Follow-Up Questions:

How do I experience the distraction of Gluttony?

What is the deeper need I am trying to meet?

What false self might be showing up?

How might I be numbing my true self?

How might Jesus meet me in the midst of Gluttony?

What might Jesus's invitation be?

How might I move from Gluttony to gratitude?

Notes:

Chapter 6

From Wrath to Waiting

John 18:1-11

When he had finished praying, Jesus left with his disciples and crossed the Kidron Valley. On the other side there was an olive grove, and he and his disciples went into it. Now Judas, who betrayed him, knew the place, because Jesus had often met there with his disciples. So Judas came to the grove, guiding a detachment of soldiers and some officials from the chief priests and Pharisees. They were carrying torches, lanterns and weapons. Jesus, knowing all that was going to happen to him, went out and asked them, "Who is it you want?" "Jesus of Nazareth," they replied. "I am he," Jesus said. (And Judas the traitor was standing there with them.). When Jesus said, "I am he," they drew back and fell to the ground. Again he asked them, "Who is it you want?"

And they said, "Jesus of Nazareth." "I told you that I am he," Jesus answered. "If you are looking for me, then let these men go." This happened so that the words he had spoken would be fulfilled: "I have not lost one of those you gave me." Then Simon Peter, who had a sword, drew it and struck the high priest's servant, cutting off his right ear. (The servant's name was Malchus.). Jesus commanded Peter, "Put your sword away! Shall I not drink the cup the Father has given me?"

Our next Deadly Sin that we will explore as an invitation to transformation is Wrath. This temptation is usually associated with anger, but it is much more than that. Anger itself may be a righteous response to injustice. God is described as being angry sometimes, with a *righteous wrath*. The difference between God's righteous displeasure with abusive injustice and our own self-righteous rage against others is that God is always redemptively working toward what he knows to be right, while we are usually fuming against what we want to be wrong. Australian Bible scholar Leon Morris argues that God's wrath is his "*strong and settled opposition to all that is evil.*"[24] Also, God's wrath is not a childish displeasure at being personally slighted. It is a broken-hearted grief for what has been carelessly ignored and damaged. Imagine this definition for God's wrath when you read these Bible passages:

---

[24] Leon Morris *The Apostolic Preaching of the Cross*, Eerdmans Pub., 1955, p. 180.

John 3:36

*Whoever believes in the Son has eternal life; whoever does not obey the Son shall not see life, but the **wrath** of God remains on him.*

Romans 1:18

*For the **wrath** of God is revealed from heaven against all ungodliness and unrighteousness of men, who by their unrighteousness suppress the truth.*

Romans 2:5

*Because of your hard and impenitent heart you are storing up **wrath** for yourself on the day of **wrath** when God's righteous judgment will be revealed.*

Romans 5:9

We have now been justified by his blood, much more shall we

be saved by him from
*the **wrath** of God.*

Ephesians 5:6
Let no one deceive you
with empty words, for
because of these things the
***wrath** of God comes*
upon the sons of
disobedience.

God is not capriciously upset because he can't have things the way he selfishly wants them. He is passionately dissatisfied with our selfish rejection of his invitation to that very loving relationship with all the things we need. His wrath is that white-hot love for his creation that motivates his sacrificial pursuit of the redemption of all things. The Deadly Sin of Wrath is our own murderous anger erupting over imagined slights against our own ideas of what we think is right. My old Regent College professor J.I. Packer writes, "*God's wrath in the Bible is never the capricious, self-indulgent, irritable, morally ignoble thing that human anger so often is. It is, instead, a right and necessary reaction to objective moral evil."*[25]

Author and teacher Rebecca Pippert wrote, "*We tend to be taken aback by the thought that God could be angry. How can a deity who is perfect and loving ever be angry? ... We take pride in our tolerance of the excesses of others. So, what is God's problem? ... But love detests what destroys the beloved. Real love stands against the deception, the lie, the sin that destroys. Nearly a century ago the theologian E.H. Glifford wrote: 'Human love here offers a true analogy: the more a father loves his son, the more he hates in him the drunkard, the liar, the traitor.' ... Anger isn't the opposite of love. Hate is, and the final form of hate is indifference ... How can a good God forgive bad people without compromising himself? Does he just play fast and loose with the facts? 'Oh, never mind ... boys will be boys'. Try telling that to a survivor of the Cambodian 'killing fields' or to someone who lost an entire family in the Holocaust.*

---

[25] J.I. Packer, *Knowing God.* IV Press., 1973, p. 136.

No. To be truly good one has to be outraged by evil and implacably hostile to injustice."[26]

In our passage in John 18, Peter is not happy with what is happening in his life. He had just had a troubling Passover meal with Jesus and the other disciples. Throughout that event Jesus had said some very confusing things: the Seder bread was Jesus's 'body'; the new relational covenant was 'in his blood'? Judas had stormed out at some point for some reason. Jesus had disrobed and washed their feet. Then they had all headed to a favourite spot in the Gethsemane garden to pray, but Peter just couldn't stay awake. Jesus was so obviously upset. Now suddenly Judas is back, but with an army troop. They're taking Jesus by force! Someone had to do something, so Peter pulls out his sword and swings it wildly with all of his passionate rage. I think it was an accident that poor Malchus's ear happened to be in the path of that sword. What a lame attempt to fix things.

---

[26] Rebecca Pippert, *Hope Has its Reasons: The Search to Satisfy Our Deepest Longings*. IV Press, 2001, p. 99-101.

Poor Peter just wanted to bring some order and justice to the scene – he wanted to protect Jesus and stop the bad people from doing bad things. This is what the deadly distraction of Wrath is. It is our flailing self-righteous false selves chopping away at others with destructive judgementalism. It is our attempts to control things with our passionate, narrow-minded weaknesses. We often think we are helping God with our self-righteous anger – but God doesn't need our help, especially when we are doing it with actions that are contrary to the very heart of God's way. I love Bono's U2 lyric: "*Stop helping God across the street like a little old lady.*"[27]

This is another way that our false selves show up. We foolishly imagine that our passionate judgement of people and circumstances is the right one. We believe that what we see someone may be doing is wrong and we have to fix it. We believe that we are right, and

[27] U2, *Stand Up Comedy*, No Line on the Horizon, 2009, Island Records, a division of Universal Music Operations Limited.

that we have to put it right. It can manifest as anger and hate, but also as a kind of twisted 'love'. The crowd's passionate adoration of Jesus on Palm Sunday turned into a destructive passion on Good Friday. Many of the same people who cried, *"Hosanna!"* on Sunday were yelling, *"Crucify him!!"* five days later. Peter was passionate for his idea of justice to be put right, but in reality he was avoiding God through his desire for security and control. My own translation of James 1:20 states, *"a human being's passion does not bring about the righteous life that God desires."*[28] Human passion should not be confused with the righteousness of God. Just because we're passionate about something doesn't make it right. How much passion one demonstrates is not a test of how spiritual one is. Passion can lead to unbridled violence. Anger and rage can lead to fights, to conflict in families, and to wars between nations. In fact undisciplined passion, even spiritual passion, even religious zeal, has

---

[28] James A. Prette, *Listening to the Challenges: A Devotional Commentary on the New Testament Letter of James.* Amazon Publishing, 2018, p. 73.

been responsible for a lot of unrighteousness in the world. People have all this human passion, all this zeal for God, and they run off and do this and that for God. And sometimes we run off ahead of God, causing all kinds of havoc.

What we are truly longing for is God's order in our lives. We are desperate for justice. We know things in this world are not right, but we take it upon ourselves to demand our ideas of rightness. Because of our fears of being wrong and out of control, and because of our wounds from being wronged, and because of our shame from being told that there is so much that is not right about us, we lash out with destructive force toward others. This destructive force is often simply an expression of our fears, shames, and wounds.

We have all done it. The point is not to feel guilty about it. It's also not about trying harder to be better. The point is to welcome Jesus into our experience of Wrath and to receive his welcoming embrace and liberating transformation. I love the image of Jesus calmly standing there in the midst of all that wrath. Jesus was peacefully loving everyone there. He loved Malchus as he gently placed his ear back on his head. He was loving Judas who had just kissed him to signal his betrayal. And he loved Peter as he tenderly said, *"Put your sword away Pete! Do you think for a moment I can't help but drink the cup the Father has given me to drink?"* I believe he was quoting from psalm 75 here.

Psa. 75:2-8

You say, "I choose the appointed time;
it is I who judge with equity.
When the earth and all its people quake,
it is I who hold its pillars firm.
To the arrogant I say, 'Boast no more,'
and to the wicked, 'Do not lift up your horns.
Do not lift your horns against heaven;
do not speak with outstretched neck.'"
No one from the east or the west
or from the desert can exalt themselves.
It is God who judges:
He brings one down, he exalts another.
In the hand of the LORD is a cup
full of foaming wine mixed with spices;

he pours it out, and all the wicked of the earth
drink it down to its very dregs.

Jesus is the one who drinks the cup of God's righteous judgement on all that is wicked and wrong in creation. He drinks it down to its very dregs, lovingly absorbing all of its poisonous wrath. While our false selves rage and arrogantly lift 'horns' (a symbol of power) and boastfully exult in our passions for what we think is right, Jesus welcomes our true selves as he offers his own passionate justice through loving sacrifice. He welcomes us all into the embrace of this healing love. Former Overseas Missionary Fellowship director and author J. Oswald Sanders said, *"Jesus drank a cup of wrath without mercy, that we might drink a cup of mercy without wrath."*[29]   14th Century English anchoress Dame Julian of Norwich wrote, *"When we, by the working of mercy and grace, be made meek and mild, we are fully safe; suddenly is the soul oned to*

---

[29]   J. Oswald Sanders, *The Incomparable Christ.* Moody Publishers, 2009, p. 204.

God when it is truly peaced in itself; for in him is found no wrath."[30]

Jesus invites us to put away our swords. He offers transformation through *waiting*. He invites our true selves to emerge through trusting in him to bring his righteous order to all that is not right with the world, and he offers us the encouraging word that we are *all right* with him. We are all right in his embrace. We can wait in his arms while he is righting all things. And we can let go of all our need to be right in all things. The way forward is through surrendering to the invitation to wait. We can wait for him to transform us so that we can be his passionate instruments of authentic love in the world. This is his transforming work of a lifetime. Polish-born American rabbi and theologian Abraham Heschel wrote, "*Many of us are willing to embark upon any adventure, except to go into stillness and to wait, to place all the wealth of wisdom in the secrecy of the*

---

[30] Julian of Norwich, *Revelations of Divine Love.* Oxford University Pres., 2015, p. 103.

soil, to sow our own soul for a seed in that tract of land allocated to every life which we call time—and to let the soul grow beyond itself. Faith is the fruit of a seed planted in the depth of a lifetime."[31]   Jesus is inviting you to plant all your longings for order and justice in the deep soil of his loving faithfulness. He is inviting you to move from Wrath to waiting.

Let's pray a welcoming prayer:

---

[31] Abraham Joshua Heschel, *Man Is Not Alone: A Philosophy of Religion.* Farrar, Straus and Giroux, 1951, p. 88, 89.

WELCOMING PRAYER

1. Welcome Wrath:

In silence, ask God to help you remember an experience of Wrath. When have you fumed? When has anger erupted? When have you wanted order and justice? When have you experienced judgementalism? When have you been frustrated in your attempts to fix what you see as wrong? When have you lashed out at others? When have you experienced the fear of being wrong and out of control? What wounds are you carrying from being wronged, and from being told that there is so much that is not right about you? *Hold that.*

2. Welcome Jesus:

In silence, wait for Jesus to meet you in your wrath. Imagine Jesus seeing you in your wrath. Where is he? How does he look at you? What does Jesus do? What might he be saying to you? *Hold that.*

3. Let Jesus welcome you:

In silence, imagine Jesus welcoming you. How does he welcome you? What might his word of loving kindness be to you? What might Jesus's invitation be in the midst of your wrath? How does he show you his unconditional love? *Hold that.*

4. Now let go:

Let go of your desire for security and control.

Let go of your desire for approval.

Let go of your desire to change situations, people, or yourself.

Open your heart to the loving presence of God and to the healing action and grace God is giving to you right now.

Follow-Up Questions:

How do I experience the distraction of Wrath?

What is the deeper need I am trying to meet?

What false self might be showing up?

How might I be numbing my true self?

How might Jesus meet me in the midst of Wrath?

What might Jesus's invitation be?

How might I move from Wrath to waiting?

Notes:

Chapter 7

From Envy to Everyone

Mark 15:1-15

Very early in the morning, the chief priests, with the elders, the teachers of the Law and the whole Sanhedrin, reached a decision. They bound Jesus, led him away and handed him over to Pilate. "Are you the king of the Jews?" asked Pilate. "Yes, it is as you say," Jesus replied. The chief priests accused him of many things. So again, Pilate asked him, "Aren't you going to answer? See how many things they are accusing you of." But Jesus still made no reply, and Pilate was amazed. Now it was the custom at the Feast to release a prisoner whom the people requested. A man called Barabbas was in prison with the insurrectionists who had committed murder in the uprising. The crowd came up and asked

Pilate to do for them what he usually did. "Do you want me to release to you the king of the Jews?" asked Pilate, knowing it was out of envy that the chief priests had handed Jesus over to him. But the chief priests stirred up the crowd to have. Pilate release Barabbas instead. "What shall I do, then, with the one you call the king of the Jews?" Pilate asked them. "Crucify him!" they shouted. "Why? What crime has he committed?" asked Pilate. But they shouted all the louder, "Crucify him!" Wanting to satisfy the crowd, Pilate released Barabbas to them. He had Jesus flogged, and handed him over to be crucified.

Our final invitation to meet Jesus in our everyday life experience is the deadly distraction of Envy. I chose to end with this one because the scripture passage I associated it with leads directly to the cross. Pilate knew that the religious leaders had handed Jesus over to be destroyed because they were envious of him (Mark 15:10). Envy is most commonly understood and experienced as jealousy. We are jealous of what others have that we do not. Unfortunately, what gets the most envious attention is what is seen on the outside – we give most of our attention to people's looks, their attributes, and their material possessions. (What usually gets neglected is what is on the inside – wisdom, maturity, and true beauty). We see what those around us have and we want it all. We also think it is unfair and unjust that anyone has anything more or better than us, and it drives us to violence: violence against self, our neighbours, the world, and God.

Proverbs 14:30 states: *"A heart at peace gives life to the body, but envy rots the bones."* Envy corrupts us from the inside out. The writer of Ecclesiastes says, *"I saw that all toil and all achievement spring from one person's envy of another. This too is meaningless, a chasing after the wind"* (Eccl. 4:4). We compete with each other for stuff and status, but it's all just worthless pursuit of the wind. Psalm 37:1 implores us to not envy those who do wrong. Later it states: *"Better is the little that the righteous have than the wealth of many wicked"* (Ps. 37:16). But it's hard not to be desirous of another's abundance, even if they got it by dishonest means. James, Peter, and Paul all mention Envy as a problem in the New Testament. Paul mentions it six times in his thirteen letters. In Philippians 1:15 he declares that some people were even preaching Christ out of envy. I know I have been jealous of other ministers. I wish I had their budgets, their buildings, their board members, and their abilities. Yes, even ministers can be competitive and petty. It is ridiculous!

In Canadian author Margaret Atwood's *A Handmaid's Tale*, the character, Offred, seeing a pregnant woman states, *"You can only be jealous of someone who has*

something you think you ought to have yourself."[32]
Though she hates her life in the oppressive Gilead society, she envies the very state in which she is entrapped. Jealousy is a monster that mocks us while it consumes us. In Shakespeare's play *Othello*, Iago tells his master,

> *O, beware, my lord, of jealousy;*
> *It is the green-eyed monster,*
> *which doth mock*
> *The meat it feeds on.*
> *That cuckold lives in bliss,*
> *Who, certain of his fate,*
> *loves not his wronger:*
> *But O, what damnèd minutes*
> *tells he o'er*
> *Who dotes, yet doubts, suspects,*
> *yet strongly loves!*[33]

And poor Othello simply replies, "*O misery!*" This is the evil trap of Envy. It is the opposite of love. 20th Century German pastor and theologian Dietrich

---

[32] Margaret Atwood, *The Handmaid's Tale*. Penguin Random House, 2019, p. 185.
[33] William Shakespeare, *Othello* Act 3, Scene 3, 165–171.

Bonhoeffer wrote, "*God's truth judges created things out of love, and Satan's truth judges them out of envy and hatred.*"[34]

We feel like we are missing out – and it's not fair! I want what you have. I believe I deserve it more than you do, and I want it now. And it escalates into violence. The chief priests, the elders, the teachers of the Law, and the whole Sanhedrin were jealous and resentful of what Jesus had – all the attention of the crowd. What Jesus also had was a perfect relationship with all things. He consistently displayed that he was in perfect harmony with natural creation, with his loving people, and with the Triune community of the Godhead. He proved his authority over the natural world. He attracted thousands of faithful followers. He declared and demonstrated his authority as the visible representation of the Living God on Earth. The religious leaders were jealous of this and so they

[34] Dietrich Bonhoeffer, *Ethics*. Macmillan Publishing Co., 1955, p. 361.

destroyed him. Pilate knew it was Envy that had driven the chief priests to hand Jesus over to him.

What we are really longing for when tempted by Envy is inclusion. We all yearn to belong within an environment of naturally ordered love. We long for a communal way of living in loving relationships together. We desire a love within our true selves that is whole and healthy. And, whether we know it or not, we ache for a right relationship with the eternal, loving God. This is exactly who Jesus was, and it is what Jesus offers us now. He was the human in perfect relationship with God. This is what we are naturally created, for and so we are desperate for it. We know that this is what is actually right, but we experience its brokenness in every way, and so we envy the goodness we observe in others' lives. We think they have it better. They have it. We resent it. We want it. We fight to get it and keep it.

This resentment escalates into a violent reduction of everything and everyone in creation to objects we expect to serve us and our pleasures. We do violence to creation when we use and abuse God's world with abandon. We also do violence to ourselves if, because of envy, we reject our unique place in this world, or if we neglect the wonderful gift God is giving through who we uniquely are and where God has placed us, or if we disregard the unique treasures of our distinctive wounds and wonders. It is violent to compare and compete with each other for what we think are scarce supplies of love and goodness in the world. And we do relational violence against God in our avoidance to respond to his invitations for love and community with everyone.

God is inviting everyone into a satisfying belonging in Holy Community. But we are distracted from all that God is offering by our envious grasping for false security and approval, and by our desire to control situations, people, and ourselves. We often fear that we are missing out on something better. We dread that we don't have enough, or that we are not enough. It feels unfair and frustrating. We have wounds from experiences of being passed over, or from being told in many ways that we don't belong, or that we don't deserve goodness. In shame we hate who we are and what we have. This leaves us insecure, lonely, deprived and detached. We live in a cloud of detachment from self, others, creation, and God with feelings of – *I am not enough, you are not enough, it is not enough, God is not enough.* We are detached and distracted by Envy. The point is not to feel guilty about it, nor to just try harder not to do it. The point is to be transformed by God right in the middle of it. The point is to turn to Jesus who is right here welcoming you into his arms again.

Centre on Jesus. Where is he in that scene with Pilate and the religious leaders? He's right there with him. He is right in the midst of those who turn on him in their violent envy. He loved them all. He stood there in the midst of their assaults with calm, silent love. Pilate was so frustrated by Jesus's silent resolve of love. While Pilate plotted and the religious leaders raged, Jesus waited in silence and welcomed their envy. He absorbed their violence. He takes it all. He takes it all to the cross. He puts it all to death. He absorbs all of our exclusive, escalating envy and offers back his inclusive welcome of everyone. He offers us forgiveness, meaning, and belonging. He offers his peace in the enough-ness of everyone and everything. He welcomes the distracted, the detached, the desperate, the dangerous. He welcomes every angry, lonely, wounded, fearful, shameful, hurting one of us.

The cross absorbs all of it – all of us. The one who has everything let go of everything to give everyone everything we need. He welcomes us all. He offers everyone the loving embrace and belonging we are looking for. He invites our true selves into his embrace, gives us everything we need, and then he invites us into an adventure of being given away – as the unique gifts we are – to the world that needs us.

You are needed. Your true self is everything that is needed. With all of your wounds and gifts, poverties and privileges, strengths and weaknesses, he makes you the perfectly unique gift that the world needs right here, right now. The way forward is to surrender to the invitation to offer yourself, just as God has made you – a gift to everyone around you. Jesus is welcoming all of your envy and offering you the invitation to move from Envy into being that special gift to everyone that your true self is meant to be.

Let's pray a welcoming prayer:

WELCOMING PRAYER

1. <u>Welcome Envy:</u>

In silence, ask God to help you remember an experience of Envy. When have you been jealous of someone? How have you been comparing and competing with others? What are you desiring right now? What do you wish was different about your life? What are you resenting? What do you fear about what is missing in your life? What are you ashamed of that is a part of who you are? What wounds are you carrying because you resent what you have or don't have? How are you feeling insecure? *Hold that.*

2. <u>Welcome Jesus:</u>

In silence, wait for Jesus to meet you in your envy. Imagine Jesus seeing you in your envy. Where is he? How does he look at you? What does Jesus do? What might he be saying to you? *Hold that.*

3. <u>Let Jesus welcome you:</u>

In silence, imagine Jesus welcoming you. How does he welcome you? What might his word of loving kindness be to you? What might Jesus's invitation be in the midst of your envy? How does he show you his unconditional love? You perfectly belong in the eternal community of Father, Son, and Holy Spirit. You are a vital part of God's family, the Church. You are the gift that your world needs right now. *Hold that.*

4. <u>Now let go:</u>

Let go of your desire for security and control.

Let go of your desire for approval.

Let go of your desire to change situations, people, or yourself.

Open your heart to the loving presence of God and to the healing action and grace God is giving to you right now.

Follow-Up Questions:

How do I experience the distraction of Envy?

What is the deeper need I am trying to meet?

What false self might be showing up?

How might I be numbing my true self?

How might Jesus meet me in the midst of Envy?

What might Jesus's invitation be?

How might I move from Envy to everyone?

Notes:

CONCLUSION

At our home church, we started this meditation on the 'Seven Invitations' on Ash Wednesday, February 26, 2020. At that Ash Wednesday evening service, we put ashes on the foreheads of those assembled in contemplation of our own mortality. We reminded each person, *"Remember you are dust, and to dust you shall return."* After that week the whole world began to change. The novel coronavirus COVID-19 ravaged the world and everything was altered. People's plans were cancelled. Schools and businesses closed. Governments ordered people to isolate indoors. Families were separated. People got sick. Many died. So much of what had been taken for granted for so long had suddenly turned to dust.

But really, none of the fundamental things of life changed at all. There were deaths and births. There was sickness and springtime. There were griefs and gifts, mortality and miracle all around us as usual. We held it all together, and we held the griefs and the gifts together. And we held it all in community together. And we were held together in the loving embrace of the Holy Community of Father, Son, and Holy Spirit.

In our Lenten Series on the Seven Deadly Sins: Pride, Greed, Lust, Sloth, Gluttony, Wrath, and Envy, we saw how these seven deadly distractions can become seven wonderful invitations. They are deadly invitations to die a little more to our selfishness and live a little more centred in love. It's not a matter of feeling guilty or trying harder. It is a matter of accepting his loving invitation to transformation.

Jesus offers us this continuing invitation to ongoing transformation. He demonstrated his authority to invite us into that journey, through the power of his enduring love over all of our deadly distractions. He absorbed all of our deadly sins in the cross. All Pride, Greed, Lust, Sloth, Gluttony, Wrath, and Envy are absorbed into the cross, which transforms these distractions into opportunities. He takes all of our distractions and relocates them in his death and resurrection. The cross and resurrection disrupt our deadly distractions and relocate us – from pride to peace, from greed to generosity, from lust to love, from sloth to sabbath, from gluttony to gratitude, from wrath to waiting, from envy to everyone.

Each distraction reminds us of our deepest longings, which are actually yearnings for connection with the loving God. He is welcoming us to hold him as we are being held by him; to hold that – then let it go in surrender to his new life in us. Here is a lovely poem by retired United Methodist minister and spiritual teacher Tod Loder which sums up so much of our meditation:

Gather Me To Be With You

O God, gather me now
*   to be with you*
*   as you are with me.*
Soothe my tiredness;
*   quiet my fretfulness;*
*   curb my aimlessness;*
*   relieve my compulsiveness;*
let me be easy for a moment.

O Lord, release me
    from the fears and guilts
        which grip me so tightly;
     from the expectations and opinions
        which I so tightly grip,
that I may be open
    to receiving what you give,
        to risking something genuinely new,
            to   learning   something   refreshingly
different.

O God, gather me
    to be with you
        as you are with me.
Forgive me
    for claiming so much for myself
        that I leave no room for gratitude;
    for confusing exercises in self-importance
        with acceptance of self–worth;
    for complaining so much of my burdens
        that I become a burden;
     for competing against other so insidiously
        that I stifle celebrating them
            and receiving your blessing through their
gifts.

O God, gather me
    to be with you
        as you are with me.
Keep me in touch with myself,
     with my needs,

my anxieties,
 my angers,
  my pain,
   my corruptions,
that I may claim them as my own
rather than blame them on someone else.

O Lord, deepen my wounds
 into wisdom;
shape my weaknesses
 into compassion;
gentle my envy
 into enjoyment,
  my fear into trust,
   my guilt into honesty,
    my accusing fingers into tickling
ones.

O God,
 gather me to be with you
  as you are with me.[35]

Let's pray a welcoming prayer:

---

[35] Ted Loder, *Guerillas of Grace, Prayers for the Battle.*
Augsburg Fortress, 1981, p. 76.

WELCOMING PRAYER

1. Welcome distraction:

In silence, ask God to help you acknowledge whatever it is that is distracting you from his love.

Hold that.

2. Welcome Jesus:

In silence, wait for Jesus to meet you in that distraction. Imagine Jesus seeing you. Where is he? How does he look at you? What does Jesus do? What might he be saying to you? *Hold that.*

3. Let Jesus welcome you:

In silence, imagine Jesus welcoming you. How does he welcome you? What might his word of loving kindness be to you? What might Jesus's invitation be in the midst of your distractions? How does he show you his unconditional love? *Hold that.*

4. Now let go:

Let go of your desire for security and control.

Let go of your desire for approval.

Let go of your desire to change situations, people, or yourself.

Open your heart to the loving presence of God and to the healing action and grace God is giving to you right now.

Notes:

Manufactured by Amazon.ca
Bolton, ON

27262159R00074